YOU HAVE THE POWER

Find Your STRENGTH and Believe You Can

LEAH WILLIAMSON

Captain of the England Women's Football Team

YOU HAVE THE POWER

Find Your STRENGTH and Believe You Can

Written with Suzanne Wrack

MACMILLAN CHILDREN'S BOOKS

Published 2023 by Macmillan Children's Books
an imprint of Pan Macmillan
The Smithson, 6 Briset Street, London EC1M 5NR
EU representative: Macmillan Publishers Ireland Ltd, 1st Floor,
The Liffey Trust Centre, 117–126 Sheriff Street Upper
Dublin 1, D01 YC43
Associated companies throughout the world
www.panmacmillan.com

ISBN 978-1-0350-2316-5

1 3 5 7 9 8 6 4 2

A CIP catalogue record for this book is available from the British Library.

Printed and bound by CPI Group (UK) Ltd, Croydon CR0 4YY
Designed by Janene Spencer

For my cousins, Henry and Athena.

For all the young girls we have opened doors for,
I hope this helps you walk through them confidently
and without hesitation. For the young boys who
support them, I hope you always choose to be an ally.

This is only the beginning of your journey.

Contents

Hello,

My name is Leah Williamson. I'm a footballer. You might have watched me lead England out onto the pitch as the team's captain at the Euros in 2022. You might have seen me lift that big silver trophy when we won the tournament. We were the first England team to win a European title. I still can't believe it!

Even now, I get goosebumps thinking about the end of that final. It was the proudest moment of my life. There had been a long journey to get to that moment, with lots of twists and turns, that involved not just us players on the pitch, but so many others. But winning the tournament wasn't the end of the journey, it was another beginning.

AND NOW WE NEED PEOPLE LIKE YOU TO CONTINUE OUR STORY.

What is the story? In part, it's the story of women and girls who have been pushed to the sidelines taking centre stage. It's a story about football, about grit and determination. But it's more than that. It's about having the freedom to find what you love and to go on to be the best you can be at it, whatever it is. I don't want that win to just inspire girls to play football, I want it to prove to all people, whatever their passion is, that they should believe in themselves and follow their dreams.

So, this isn't a book about how to be a good footballer – (though it does include some tips and tricks I've learnt along the way!):

THIS IS A BOOK ABOUT FINDING OUT WHAT MAKES YOU HAPPY, WHATEVER THAT MAY BE.

It's a book about finding your inner strength, believing in yourself and taking control of your life. It's full of lessons that helped me along the way, things I wish I'd learned at your age, and I'm still learning how to bring our the best in myself and other.

Playing lots of football hasn't just developed my skills on the pitch. The things you learn while playing – teamwork, organisation, determination – are just as important when the ninety minutes are up. So, whether reading this book makes you want to put on some trainers and go play a kickabout with your friends or not, I hope it will give you the skills to succeed in all kinds of things!

One thing I love about being part of a team is energising those around me to thrive and be happy. I've played in lots of teams over the years, but it would be the biggest honour to be a part of your team – which includes your friends, your family, your teachers – because I want to help you be the happiest version of yourself. I want to help you achieve anything you want to, I want to show you that you have the power. All you have to do, is read on.

It's time to begin.

Leah

Do What You Love

When I was growing up, lots of people thought girls weren't interested in football. I never really understood why.

For as long as I can remember, I have **LOVED** football.

I can't tell you when I started loving football, but I can tell you why – my family loves football. They always have, and that's why I loved football too, right from the moment I understood what it was. (And probably even before then!) We shared it as a passion.

FOOTBALL WAS WHAT BROUGHT US TOGETHER AS A FAMILY.

My brother Jacob is five years younger than me, which meant that we lived quite different lives, but football was the one thing that we always had in common. We'd play in the garden all the time, and sometimes our parents would take us to Regent's Park in London where we'd put our jumpers down as goalposts and have a game of footie, two-on-two. It was always a good battle!

Football also divided our house. You see, my mum is a massive Arsenal fan, but my dad is an avid Tottenham supporter – and they're Arsenal's biggest rivals! My mum was determined that I would be an Arsenal supporter like her. There was **NO WAY** she was going to let my dad recruit me to

Tottenham (he did try though). When I was five, he took me to a match at White Hart Lane, Tottenham's stadium. We said goodbye to mum and headed to London. Before we went into the stadium, my dad bought me a Tottenham shirt for me to change into – my mum would never let me wear one so he had to be sneaky about it! It was a really fun day, but it only took one trip to see The Arsenal and I was sold. There are loads of things that are great about Arsenal, but the main reason I loved it was because I went with my mum and my grandma. When I went to watch Tottenham with my dad – I didn't feel out of place, but I was aware of being a girl surrounded by boys and men. So being able to share football with my mum and grandma at Arsenal games felt very special. I've loved Arsenal ever since. I've always felt at home there.

My dad won my brother over to Tottenham though – disaster! – but it meant we had a good fun rivalry at home.

From an early age, my family instilled in me that it's important to do what you love, and follow your passions. Football was that passion for me. Not just watching it but playing it too, even though it hasn't always been an easy journey.

Not many people know this, but when I was small I didn't walk properly. My toes pointed inwards instead of straight forward. When your feet point inwards like that it's called 'in-toeing' or being 'pigeon-toed'. To help correct it, I've had to wear insoles in my shoes my whole life. The doctors said I should try gymnastics or horse riding, as they might help to make my feet straighter and could help me avoid having to wear a brace on the back of my legs. So, I started gymnastics lessons when I was two years old. That meant going to the gym just down the road from my grandma's house four evenings a week. I did gymnastics right up until I started in the Arsenal academy when I was nine, at which point it got too difficult to do both. Ironically, it was doing gymnastics that developed my interest in playing football!

My gymnastics coach loved football, and at the end of every session on Friday, if we finished a little early and were waiting for our parents to pick us up, he would get out a football and we would kick it about. It was brilliant because everyone would get involved. Gymnastics is an individual sport, but when we played football together at the end of the sessions I got a taste for what it would be like to be a part of a team; working together to achieve something. I already loved my team at home, my family, and now I had an idea of what it was like to be a part of a team outside of that family unit.

After one of those chaotic fun sessions I went home and asked my dad if I could have a goalpost for the garden for my birthday – and he got me one! As soon as I had a goal, I was out playing football as much as possible – with my brother, my mum, my dad, even my grandma!

Getting that goal changed my life. It meant that football was always on my radar, and I was always running outside to play, whenever I could. Not long after getting the goal I told my mum that I wanted to join a team and play regularly – I didn't want to just do it now and again at the end of gymnastics. She was a little concerned about it, because she used to play football when she was younger and knew what it was like for girls. (I will tell you more about that later.)

I LOVE FOOTBALL

But I really, really loved football, and I wasn't going to let anything stop me from playing – not the fact that I was a girl, nor the fact that my feet turned in! All I knew was that I loved the sport and I wanted to play as much as possible.

Sometimes it was tough. I was self-conscious because I felt like I wasn't what they expected a football player to look like, and not just because I was a girl, but because I was a bit lanky, or my knees were too knobbly.

Sometimes I felt as though I wasn't quick enough, or skilful enough. I would also get injured more easily. For a very long time I put the everyday insoles that my doctor advised me to wear in my normal shoes into my football boots as well. They weren't designed for sport, but I didn't know that at the time. I didn't realize that the reason I was getting so many ankle injuries was because the insoles raised my foot on one side – by the time I was twenty-two I'd already had six major ankle injuries!

I haven't let any of this stop me. It's meant I've had to work harder. I've had to convince coaches and players that I am just as good as any other player. Even though my ankles are weak and I have long legs, which is really unusual for the position I play (I'm a defender, and they're usually strong and muscular, whereas I'm more long and skinny). I've learned to make all of these things my strengths.

All of our weaknesses can be strengths at times and that's what gives you an edge. It's what makes you different. I've had commentators call me 'Bambi' before, because my legs are so long and they see it as a weakness. But when we're doing a rondo training (where we are in a circle with two players in the middle trying to win the ball, as we pass it around), I'll stick my toe out and because my legs are long and lanky I'll block a ball easily. We're all different in how we're made and the different things we can do – make what's special about you, work for you!

If you think about great footballers, you might think about those who can do fancy tricks and skills. Cool skills are not my strengths, but I'm not ashamed to have different strengths to others. In fact, having eleven players with different strengths is the key to being a winning team. If everyone on the pitch was good at shooting, but there were no good tacklers or dribblers, the team wouldn't get very far. But a team that has a mix of different strengths, with some players who can run really fast, others who can jump very high, and some who can pass really well, will be much stronger. And that's a rule for life, not just football. We all have different skills, and that's what means we can work together better as a team.

IT'S SO IMPORTANT TO FIND THE THINGS THAT YOU LOVE TO DO.

I love football because it has always offered me so much. It gave me a chance to challenge what was considered to be 'normal' and to do things that some people didn't think I should do. It gave me an opportunity to learn what it's like to be a fighter; to shout back at all those people who think women and girls shouldn't play football, just by doing it. I have learned the power of coming together and being part of a team and a movement.

I was always made to feel like I could do anything. Whenever anyone in my family wanted to try something, they did it, and they were supported by everybody. My parents never questioned what I wanted to do. Even if what I wanted to do wasn't always as common for girls, or I was too small, or my feet made things difficult. And I'm so grateful for that. My mum and dad were my first teammates, helping me to be the best I could be, at anything and everything I wanted to do. I loved football because it made me confident, it helped me to communicate really well with others, and kept me fit and healthy, and also because it was another way of spending time and sharing a passion with my family.

My mum and dad are my biggest cheerleaders. They helped me to believe that I could do anything I wanted – that I was in charge – and I had the ability to be great at anything. And my brother has always been my biggest supporter. He has seen me playing football his whole life, and always encouraged me. That is why you will always see me celebrating with my mum, my dad and my little brother after I've won something, because without them, I wouldn't be where I am today.

Everyone's lives looks very different, but every single one of you reading this book matters. I know that I was so lucky to have my family believing in me, but even if you feel like you don't have a solid support system around you, I want you to know that you can find a way to do what you love. Your parents, guardians, siblings, friends, teachers, are all around you, there for you to turn to if you need help.

And if you don't feel like you have a group of cheerleaders around you telling you that you can do anything, I want you to be your own best cheerleader. You are the single most important cheerleader that you will have in your life.

 I want you to believe that you can do anything.

 I want you to love yourself.

 I want you to never feel alone in feeling different.

Being **DIFFERENT** is about being unique, it's what makes you, you. **YOU** are special.

Sharing passions and hobbies is important, but it is also really important that you focus on the things that YOU love to do and to spend time exploring what you like and don't like. And your passion doesn't have to be football – it could be anything! It's important to spend the time to find out what makes you happy. Take the things that you were brought up around and love as your starting point, but also explore beyond that. Because spending time doing what you love makes you happier. That's a scientific fact. It takes your mind off your worries, it relaxes you and it makes you better in other areas of your life.

At the stage you are in your life now, it's likely that everything will feel like it's changing pretty quickly. Every decision you make will feel hugely important, every argument you have with friends or every test you fail might make you feel like your world is ending. But it's not.

FAR FROM IT.

YOUR LIFE IS JUST STARTING.

And a good way to remind you of what it feels like to have fun and be happy is to have something to do that gives you joy and reminds you that there is more to life than what you've been worrying

about. For me, that was football. For you, it could be a sport, or it could be art, it could be maths, it could be music. There are so many options!

It also doesn't have to be something that becomes your job. Football was a hobby for me right up until I signed my first contract with Arsenal. My mum made sure I always treated football as a hobby because she wanted me to stay passionate about it, and because I was passionate, it never became a chore. I never, ever turned up to training because I had to. I turned up because it was fun and I *wanted* to.

When I started playing with the senior side at Arsenal, I had the opportunity to move into a club house and live with the other players, but I didn't want to do that because it would have meant that football became my whole life. I didn't want that – I wanted football to be my escape.

Keeping football as a passion meant that I was focused on turning up, being the best version of myself and having fun. Having hobbies that help you relax, have fun and escape from stress is so important. Now that playing football is my job, even though I still love it, I make sure that I have other passions that help take my mind off of it when I need to and other interests outside of football.

Doing what you love is important for your own wellbeing, but it is also important for the people and world around you too. If you're doing something that makes you unhappy, why would you smile at the person walking past you in the street? Why would you open a door for someone? Why would you pick up someone's dropped shopping? If you are doing something you love, you will feel good about yourself and you will project that out into the world. The happier you are, the better a place the world will be.

Like I said, when I was growing up it wasn't considered normal for girls to like football. But I always just thought, what does it even mean to be 'normal'? Who gets to decide what is normal and what isn't? And why is being normal something we should try to be anyway?

IT'S MUCH COOLER TO BE DIFFERENT.

Not all of the activities or sports or films or music you enjoy will be the most popular, and there is nothing wrong with that. Having different styles and different tastes is what makes you unique from everyone else. When I was a kid, I liked being different, and I still like being different now. I do the things that make me happy. If you are being different, it means you are focused on doing what **YOU** want to do and what makes you happy, rather than doing what other people want you to do.

When you find the thing that you love you start to find out who you are as a person. You avoid doing things that other people do, just because you think they're 'cool'. I know it can be hard not to care what people think about you. If anyone makes you feel uncool for doing something you love, like playing football, I'd feel sorry for them, because it means that they are probably spending a lot of time trying to fit in and not much time finding out what they love to do.

FIND WHAT YOU'RE INTERESTED IN,

AND IT WILL ENRICH YOU.

The earlier you can work out who you are as a person, understand what makes you feel good, and be comfortable with your choices, the more fun you will have.

I'm not trying to make you the next Lauren Hemp with this book (what a player!), but hopefully I can help you feel good in yourself and your choices and help you have fun. Everything that I do in my life, I do regardless of what people will think about it. That gives me a lot of freedom. I am still learning every single day, but I know that every choice or decision I make is made for me, and not to try and fit in or be someone I'm not.

That is what I want you to strive to be. You are capable of so much. You have so much learning and growing to do. But that should not be a stressful thing, it should be exciting, and it should be fun!

Did you know that we use fewer muscles to smile than we do to frown? That means it's actually MORE effort to frown than it is to smile! If you are doing something that you love, life is easier.

Being able to do what you love is a luxury and you should grab it with both hands. Plenty of people don't have that luxury – in some countries women can't even go and watch football in stadiums, let alone play football! But also, life is only so long, so why would you not try to spend every minute trying to enjoy it?

[2]

Yes We Can

When I was six years old I was desperate to play football, but it wasn't easy for my parents to find a team for me to join. It was hard for girls to play football back then – much harder than it is now. Because football had traditionally been seen as a sport for boys, there weren't many teams I could join as a girl.

Now, there are so many more girls' teams and sessions for girls to join – which is amazing! Mixed football teams, with boys and girls playing together, are also a lot more common.

When I was growing up there were plenty of boys' teams around, but the problem was that not many of the coaches wanted a girl playing in their teams. Some would make up an excuse by saying that their teams were full and there was no space for me. While no one told me 'no' to my face, it felt like I wasn't entirely welcome.

Eventually, my mum reached out to a local coach, who she had gone to school with. He coached a boys' team called Bletchley Scot Youth, and he said I could join the team if I was good enough. He was very clear that he wasn't going to take me just because I was a girl, and also that he wasn't *not* going to take me just because I was a girl, either! His attitude was:

AS LONG AS SHE'S GOOD ENOUGH, SHE CAN PLAY.

Of course, I was nervous. Starting something new and unknown is always a bit scary, and being a girl trying to get into a boys' team only made that feeling worse. But I also knew that I could do it. And, more than that, I really **WANTED** to do it. All that was in my head was:

I WANT TO PLAY FOOTBALL AND THIS IS THE ONLY WAY THAT I CAN DO IT.

It's hard to describe how much confidence I took away from the very first session with Scot Youth. Despite how nervous I was before I turned up, I knew from the first moment I touched the ball that I could do it – that I could play – and that made me feel great.

One thing that really sticks out in my mind is the match we played at the end of that first training session. At half-time, I was switched from one team to the other. At first I worried I was in trouble, but actually I had scored so many goals my coach put me on the other team to even things out.

It didn't matter that I was the only girl surrounded by boys, because I just felt so good. And when doing something you love makes you feel that good, it's hard to not feel a sense of belonging. It felt like me and football were meant to be.

The other kids at Scot Youth made me feel accepted straight away, but often when we played in matches, I was made to feel like I didn't belong by the team we were playing against. The parents of boys on the other teams would often scream things like:

'GET THE GIRL!' OR 'GET HER!'

Parents were encouraging their boys to play hard against me and potentially hurt me, just because I was a girl.

HOW BAD IS THAT?

I don't know why they did that, but I guess they just didn't like that their son was being outplayed by a girl.

I used to get a bit nervous when parents shouted things like that because I thought my mum and dad might get angry at them for it. My mum would worry about me getting hurt too. The boys from the other teams would sometimes tackle me viciously, I think because they were so panicked about losing to a girl. My parents made me wear a gumshield in my mouth to protect my teeth for the whole year I played in that boys' team. It was so embarrassing. As if I didn't already stand out enough! But it was worth it, because it meant I got to play.

When I was six, I didn't have to worry about different changing rooms or sports bras or anything like that, though I did have to buy boys' football boots because football boots for girls didn't exist! I only started to notice the physical differences between me and the boys when I was a little bit older, in years seven and eight at school, when we started playing in football tournaments that had both girls and boys in. Even then, although the fastest boy would often be faster than the fastest girl, you could always compete as a girl because at that age your size and differences aren't that great. You also very quickly forget about any differences when you're playing because you aren't playing one-on-one. You're a team, working together, competing together, and having fun.

I've always felt confident in my body and my physicality, and that came from having started gymnastics at such a young age. It's weird, I went to gymnastics to help correct my feet, and trying to fix that problem is what ended up making me so physically confident overall.

For me, P.E. was the best time of the week at school. When I was in primary school a lot of people liked P.E., but once I was in secondary school that started to change. I was used to doing lots of different sports and knew how much fun you could have running around. That helped me understand that P.E. could be fun and enjoyable, but there were lots of things that could have put me off too.

There are probably times when you've not wanted to do P.E. Our bodies change when we're in secondary school and we might become more self-conscious about how we look, how we smell, how we feel and how we move. Have you ever felt like that? If so, let me tell you: you are not alone. All these things can change our relationship with sport, and often it can feel like no one is willing to talk about it. When I was at school, we didn't talk about why P.E. can actually be a good thing to do for someone who is on their period (because it improves blood circulation which can help ease period pains!) and we didn't talk about how people on their periods could comfortably take part in sport.

For example, when you have P.E. at school, do you have access to showers? If you do, does anyone ever use them? We had showers but nobody ever felt comfortable using them, and we were never encouraged to either. That was pretty off-putting. Especially when we had P.E. at the start of the day, because no one wants to be smelly and sweaty all day!

There are so many things that can make you not want to do sport. I loved sport and there were times when even I was put off doing P.E., just because I didn't know what to do with my body. But I don't ever want you to feel this way.

You have a voice, and I want you to be empowered to feel like you can talk about changes that could make P.E. more fun for everybody. And I can tell you, I bet your teachers would want to hear what you have to say. Do you know why? Because physical exercise actually improves your brain's health. So if you're doing physical exercise, then it's easier for you to concentrate, and you'll perform better in other classes!

No matter how shy or self-conscious you are, if you embrace your best sweaty self in P.E. and push past those fears, you will have **FUN**. So much fun. And it doesn't even have to be P.E. – there are so many different ways that you can get moving, whether it's walking, running, swimming, team sports . . . the possibilities are endless! There are so many things out there for you to try, and I promise you that once you find your way to connect with movement, you won't look back. Look at me – if I hadn't had to do gymnastics as a kid, I might never have discovered my passion for playing football!

I was lucky because my passion for sport helped me to push past any feelings of self-consciousness. I found that once you're having fun, you don't care so much about what you look like because you are too busy enjoying yourself. I was also lucky because I was positively influenced by parents, especially the women in my family. For as long as I can remember, my grandma has played badminton weekly and my mum loves sport. So, when I went to school, I already had confidence in myself and my body, and thought of sport as something girls and women did all the time.

Even though I was only at Scot Youth for a year, I learned so much from playing in that team. I discovered how to push past being nervous, and learned how to be brave. I learned that great things can happen when you take risks and try something new. No matter how scared you are when you start something new, or how strange it feels when you don't see anyone else who looks like you, you can do it.

YOU CAN BE BRAVE

YOU CAN PUSH YOURSELF OUTSIDE OF YOUR COMFORT ZONE

YOU BELONG

Pushing yourself to do something that you've been a bit nervous about trying can do so much for you. It can make you feel great about yourself. Even the smallest achievement, can make you feel on top of the world.

Through sport I've learned to try not to compare myself to everyone else. I know that it can be hard – we all look at the people around us and can't help but feel like we're better or worse than them at all sorts of different things. But it's important to remember that:

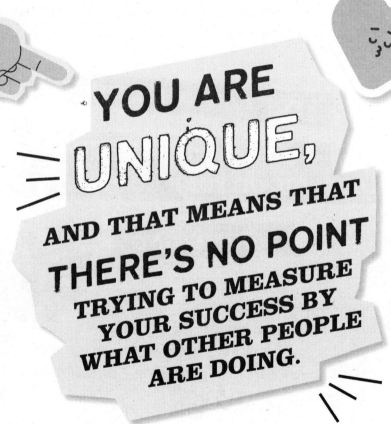

YOU ARE UNIQUE, AND THAT MEANS THAT THERE'S NO POINT TRYING TO MEASURE YOUR SUCCESS BY WHAT OTHER PEOPLE ARE DOING.

At your age, you are also developing at a different rate to your friends. That means that your best friend might be a little bit taller than you, or a faster reader than you are, but by next year, it could be the other way around – for no reason, other than the fact that your developmental timeline is different to theirs! That's why it's important to prioritise being in competition with yourself, and to understand what your own expectations of yourself are. Being in competition with other people will only push you so far, because their top standard is different from your own. But being in competition with yourself will push you to be better over and over again, and raise your bar as high as **YOU** want it to be!

When I was at school, I used to find it frustrating and a little upsetting that some of my friends stopped playing sports, just because they didn't feel comfortable doing it while their bodies were starting to change. Lots of them hadn't had the chance to play sport like I had and didn't know all of the good things you get out of it. I became the person who would rally people into getting involved in P.E., and who would try and get my friends to join me. I wanted them to feel the way that I felt doing P.E., I wanted them to discover what almost seemed to be a secret. And I want you to discover that secret too.

If you give sport and P.E. a go, I promise that you will benefit from it in so many ways.

Even if it's not your main interest, it can be so helpful to enjoy doing a range of things. Just because your main interest is maths or art, it doesn't mean that you can't enjoy football, too!

I know it can be frustrating. How and when your body will change is completely out of your control, and while your body is changing, you may notice that you're not improving at sport as quickly as you like. But I promise you, it's worth sticking with sport and pushing through the times where it gets tough. Try to focus on what you can control, and the things you can work on, like your technique, learning new skills and teamwork.

THE MORE YOU GIVE TO SPORT, THE MORE YOU GET OUT OF IT.

You can build great relationships with teachers and coaches, and having had a good run around will help you to switch off from all the stresses of the school day. My P.E. teachers saw that I had potential, but they were invested in me because I was invested in sport, not because I was good. If I couldn't throw a ball two metres, my P.E. teachers wouldn't have cared, they would have given me the same support because they could tell that I was trying. That was a good lesson – I learned that the more I put into sport, the more I got out of it, and the more my teachers wanted to help me achieve. In every subject at school, you will find that the more you put in, the more your teachers will invest their time and energy in helping you to be the best you can be.

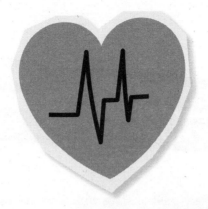

THE MORE YOU DO SPORT, THE MORE YOU LEARN ABOUT YOUR BODY, TOO.

If I was on my period, I would feel terrible, but going out and playing football made me feel better. Like I said, physical activity can even help alleviate some of the symptoms that come with periods. It also can keep you feeling fit and healthy generally.

The biggest thing that made me not walk away from P.E. and sports when I was in secondary school though, was that I had found out very early on that I **NEVER** regretted doing it.

No matter how cold or wet it was, no matter how tired or uncomfortable I felt, I have never, in my entire life, done a sports session and regretted it afterwards. Instead, I always feel amazing. That is what I tried to get across to my friends who weren't interested or were feeling self-conscious, and that is what I want to get across to you now. If you get involved in physical activity of some kind it will make you feel good about yourself. Even now, I sometimes go to training and just want it to end, but as soon as the session is over I feel great. As you get older, many people realize that one of the best ways to improve your physical and mental health is to exercise. So why not get a head start on that while you're young?

P.E. and sport should be a safe space for us all. A safe environment where nobody judges us for the way we look, the sweat patches under our arms or the hair that's out of place. If you are all having fun, you won't even notice those things.

The relationships that you make with people, the skills that you learn from being in a team (or just sweating alongside a friend!) are invaluable. There is no bad side to being active. The important thing for you to know is that sport is for you; it's there for you to try, it is there for you to fall in love with and it is there to make you feel mentally and physically better. Whether it's competitive or just for fun, sport is there to be whatever you want it to be. So give it a try!

[3]

Get Out of Your Comfort Zone

I hate losing. I'd be a pretty rubbish football player if I didn't! But, even though I hate it, I like to think that I'm a good loser.

My mum always taught me to be humble in defeat. She always said that she would be proud of me, no matter what, as long as I had tried my best and given it everything. So, no matter how frustrated I might get during a poor performance, I always turn off that frustration after the game. I will always, **ALWAYS** go and shake the hands with the players on the other team, because I want to be respectful of their achievements. Then, I'll move on.

I have to move on quickly for my own wellbeing, but that's something I've learnt to do over the years. Playing for the team you support and love is *really* mentally draining. I had always put so much pressure on myself to perform on the pitch because I cared so much about whether we won or lost. To know that *my* performance could be the difference between my team – my mum's team AND my grandparents' team – winning or losing is really scary. I used to be so terrified of losing that it affected how much I enjoyed playing. How wild is that? I was doing the thing I loved: playing football for the team I have always supported, but I was *so* scared of failing whilst I was doing it. And that meant I wasn't having fun.

There's a quote from a song that I really like which says: 'Nobody wins afraid of losing'. (Ok, ok, it's from a country song, called *Starting Over* by a country musician I like, called Chris Stapleton – who Adele loves too! See, country is cool!) I love this line. It means that if you are too scared of failing and spend too much time worrying about what might happen if you lose, you will be much less likely to win.

The closer I got to the Arsenal senior team, the more worried I was about whether I would be good enough on the pitch. There were so many times when I would walk out before a game afraid of not being good enough. I was scared that even if I had a good game, I wasn't going to reach my full potential. I actually got to a point where I started wishing away my career and thinking: 'At least I won't have to deal with losing when I retire.' I was twenty-two and I had gone from loving football, to wishing it away.

All that worrying did was make me uptight and anxious. I would put so much pressure on not wanting to fail during games that I would just end up having average performances, because I wasn't taking any risks. After all, if I was already nervous and worrying about my performance, then I probably wasn't even going to *attempt* the 40-yard diagonal pass across the pitch to set up a goal. I wasn't bad but I was only ever a six out of ten. I wasn't anywhere near reaching my full potential as a player. I wasn't pushing myself or taking the risks needed to have the great performances you need to beat the very best teams. Pushing yourself to be the best often means trying things that might not always work out, but sometimes the bigger the risk, the bigger the reward.

If you are too scared of trying new things because you're worried you might fail, you may never reach your full potential.

I want to give you an example of this: in 2018, I played in the FA Cup final at Wembley. It was Arsenal versus Chelsea, and I was *so* nervous before the game. It was a London derby (derbies are games against your local rivals) and Chelsea were the favourites to win. The team had fought hard during the season and managed to get to the final. It was a **HUGE** moment for us.

Even getting to the final was an amazing achievement and it should have been a brilliant ninety minutes for the whole team to go through together. But I hated every second of that game. I was so nervous and I really felt the pressure of the team needing to win, and that made me play terribly. I got in the changing room at half-time and I wished I could just go home. To be honest, the team as a whole wasn't at its best. Maybe we were all feeling too afraid of losing to really push ourselves to go for it. And I know I contributed to that. We ended up losing 3-1 to Chelsea.

Four years later, I was back at Wembley lifting the European championship trophy. In the years between the FA Cup final and the Euros final, I learnt so much about myself and about what makes me a good player.

Losing against Chelsea ended up being a huge moment for me – it made me realize that I had to learn to push myself, to get out of my comfort zone. I had to learn how not to worry about the result or putting in a poor performance, and I had to understand how to move on from those things if they did go wrong. I needed to learn how to walk onto the pitch, unafraid of losing. And as soon as I could learn how to do all of that, I would be in the best possible place mentally to do my best, try my hardest and take risks. *Then* I'd be more likely to contribute to my team winning. Who knows if I'd have ever dealt with that Euros final the way that I did, if I hadn't had that experience of defeat in 2018?

Getting out of my comfort zone has made me a better player. And I can tell you, when the England manager Sarina Wiegman asked me to be England captain, I had no idea it was coming! I had only played for six minutes of tournament football for the senior team, at the Women's World Cup in 2019, so I couldn't believe it when she asked me to be captain. It was just before the start of the Euro 2022 tournament, and I was only twenty-five years old – way younger than lots of the other players on the team. Sure, there was a lot of pressure. It was a big responsibility to take on. But I wasn't nervous.

I trusted the process
and I trusted myself.
I could do this.

Being the captain of an international squad is a lot of pressure. It was my first start for England at a major tournament and I would be leading the team out and wearing the captain's armband. It was at Old Trafford, an iconic stadium, in front of 68,871 fans, including my family.

I would do anything for the team, and if your manager asks you to do something because they think it will be good for the team, you do it. Your manager saying that they trust you with the armband means a lot.

Looking back now, after everything we've achieved, I sometimes wonder what would have happened if I had let the fear of losing stop me from saying yes. Accepting the captaincy was a risk, if we had been knocked out of the group stage at the Euros, I might have been known as the worst England captain of all time! But we ended up winning the whole thing. Taking the risk paid off. Lifting the trophy with Millie Bright was a moment I will never forget.

Winning the tournament has opened up so many opportunities for our team. It's started us all on such an amazing journey.

When I was just starting out on my football journey, I was too scared to take risks. But if you don't take risks, ones where you push yourself to try or do something that might not work out, then you'll not perform at your best. You will be holding back from trying the things that could improve your performance. Think about it – would you want to live your life going along in a straight line, where nothing really bad ever happens but nothing outstanding happens? Or would you rather be travelling along a wavy line, where there are high points and low points, but the lows make the highs all the sweeter and more valued?

Learning to play without fear, trusting my instincts and taking risks has been so important to me getting better, both as a football player and as a person. Yes, a risky pass might not get to where I want it to go. I could fail. But if it does work out, the rewards are worth the risk. You can either sit in a little comfortable zone, where you never try anything new or risky, or you can go in feeling free, not letting your nerves control you, and see what happens. It's so important for you to take risks and believe in yourself, because we get better at things with practice and hard work, but a lot of the time we learn the most from failing.

I LEARNT TO MOVE PAST MY NERVES BY STOPPING IGNORING THEM.

Instead, I started talking about them. When the Covid-19 pandemic put us into lockdown I began speaking to a psychologist. I had thought that my nerves were normal, that was just the way it would be forever, that it was something I could never change. You may think that anxiety is all in your head, but it can also provoke a physical reaction too. My anxiety used to get so high that it would affect my vision so that I couldn't see the colours of the bibs we wore in training, and other things like that. It was pretty scary.

But then I was introduced to Kate Green, who was a sports psychologist for England and Team GB. And the first thing she said to me was:

We can fix this.

I don't think I really believed her at first. I had tried to speak to a therapist before and it hadn't clicked but Kate's advice was very practical and I liked that. It suited me.

I used to suffer from performance anxiety, which means I used to get nervous and stressed out when I had a big event coming up. One of the things that Kate taught me to do to help with that feeling was focus on my breathing whenever that happened. I found that by thinking about my breathing, rather than the situation I was in, really helped.

Another technique she told me to try was to count out five positive things about myself on my hand, one finger at a time. The reason you get anxious about things is often because your brain is running through all of the negatives about the situation. But why wouldn't you just focus on the positives?

At first I didn't think it would work, because it's such a simple thing to do. But it really did. It still does. Even now, whenever I have a wave of anxiety, I go through my five things on my hand: I'm a good passer, I'm athletic, I'm quick, I'm a good communicator, and I'm kind.

If you ever feel stressed out, or like your emotions are getting too much to bear, I want you to try it. Your positives can be anything, and they can change as much as you want them to. When you're looking at your fingers and counting through your positives one at a time, it starts to feel more real. And that helps you to feel like you have more power over your situation.

It can be hard to find the right person to talk to about your feelings. It doesn't have to be a psychologist or health professional – it could be a friend, a teacher, a coach, a parent or a sibling. But once you've found the right person or people to talk to, it can make a big difference. I had spoken to other psychologists before, but Kate was the right fit for me. She helped me to realize that being nervous and vulnerable were not bad things. Speaking to someone about your worries is not a weakness. It takes strength to try to better yourself and to deal with negative thoughts.

It's important to look after your mental health as much as your physical health. Think about it – if your stomach hurt you would take medicine or see a doctor, so why wouldn't you do things to protect your mind?

Fear held me back, but it doesn't need to hold you back. You will be the best version of yourself if you can understand all the things that hold you back from giving your all, and learn to move past them.

Now, I can handle those nervous feelings. My attitude before a match is: this is an opportunity, and nobody knows what will happen. I understand that even though there are so many things that could go wrong, they are all completely out of my control. Instead, I choose to focus on the positives, on the things I want to go right. That's how I deal with both winning and losing.

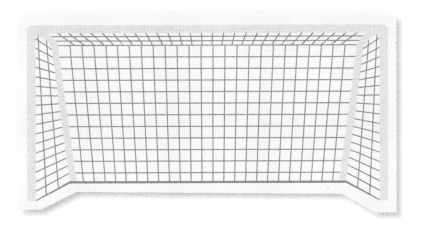

Once, I wished away the big moments, the ones where the stakes are highest (like the cup finals or matches against big rivals). Now I embrace them. I was worried that by switching off after a loss, and choosing to not dwell on what had happened, I was missing my competitive edge. But, to be honest, all that dwelling on the losses did was drain me emotionally. And then I would have to do it all again after the next game, getting more and more drained. Now, whenever I lose, I focus on what my team needs, and what can be done better next time. That way, I'm trusting myself and giving as much as I can to the team.

I have learnt that my voice is important, and that what I have to say matters. And that was just as true before I was a captain as it is now. A captain's job isn't to speak for others. It's to show them the power and value of their own voice, and to encourage them to speak up. My main goal is to help others – like you – to realize that they have power too.

Being a captain is a very social role. But I wasn't always the most comfortable in social situations. I appeared outgoing and friendly but would sometimes worry about how I was going to keep a conversation going. I would worry that I wasn't the best at welcoming new people and wasn't sure about how I came across to others. That's something I've worked on and feel more confident about now.

That's why you should always try to push yourself out of your comfort zone, because the more you do it, the easier it gets. And then you can move onto conquering your next challenge. Are you scared of talking to new people? If you are, why not try to introduce yourself to five new people at school and then have a think about how much better you were at it once you've done the fifth? How has pushing yourself to do something different made you feel? Does it still feel challenging? It doesn't have to be meeting new people. Think of something you find hard. It could be trying new foods, starting a new hobby, playing a new sport, talking about your feelings more. Can you use that to think of a way to test yourself? Even though I still struggle to talk to new people I still force myself to do it. That's one way I push myself.

If you give up before you've even started something, you have lost before you've even begun. You're not even giving yourself the chance of success. Don't do yourself that injustice.

BACK YOURSELF. BELIEVE IN YOURSELF.

Remember: vulnerability is not a weakness, it's a strength. The more you put yourself out there, take risks and give things a try, the greater the rewards will be.

[4]

Resilience, Keeping Calm & Bouncing Back

You might say I'm lucky. I've not had one injury that has kept me away from the pitch for a whole season like other players have. Chloe Kelly – who scored the winning goal in the final of the Euros! – was out for eight months with an ACL injury (Anterior Cruciate Ligament injury, which is a tear of one of the ligaments in the knee) and only just made it back in time for the big competition. Beth Mead, who was player of the tournament and won the Golden Boot for scoring the most goals, has an ACL injury that could mean she will miss some really important games. I have, however, had seven ankle injuries over the last eight years. Each time, I've been out for two-to-five months and that time can add up pretty quickly.

I was seventeen years old when I made it into the Arsenal senior team, and I was the youngest player in the squad! Moving from the junior team to the senior team was quite scary (it almost felt like starting a new school!) but even though I was nervous and worried a lot about how well I was doing, I seized the opportunity. You can be the best footballer in the world, but the stars must align for you too – which means you need a big slice of luck to get your chance, whether it's someone else moving teams or you fitting into the manager's system. You have to be given your opportunity to shine, and then you have to perform.

At the start of 2015 I was named England's Youth Player of the Year and then the Professional Footballers' Association Young Player of the Year. But a year after I started playing, I snapped my ankle and I had to take four months out to recover. Once I was back, I played my first game against Birmingham. It felt amazing to be back on the pitch after all that time. Then, in the next game, which was in the League Cup against Watford, I scored my first goal of the season. It was only my third-ever Arsenal goal – you don't get the opportunity to shoot that often as a defender! But that happiness was short-lived. I then tore ligaments in my other ankle. I missed eleven games and almost five months of a six-month season.

I was plucked out of the Arsenal Academy and walked into the First Team dressing room a lot earlier than I thought I would. I scored my first goal and was winning awards. I was where I wanted to be. And then, all of a sudden, I was injured and I couldn't play. I felt like I was going to fall off the face of the earth. I was devastated. During that recovery time, I just kept thinking, 'nobody's going to remember who I am.' I was so *so* scared that I was going to lose momentum and everyone would forget all of the hard work I'd done to earn a spot on the senior team and launch my career.

While I was injured, I was obsessed with time and getting back on the pitch. All I wanted to do was tick the boxes I needed to tick to get there: seeing doctors, doing physio, getting back on the grass, keeping my fitness up in the gym … **tick, tick, tick, tick.**

But worrying about all of that was actually a waste of my time and energy. I just needed to trust the process and trust myself – I knew I could play football, and I knew that all the work I had put in wouldn't just disappear whilst I was out injured. I just had to trust that the people around me knew what was best for my recovery, and trust that I would put in the work to get back, fighting fit.

Would I come back and be the same player? It didn't matter. I had only played for a year. I hadn't had the chance to properly prove myself yet. I was still young (even if eighteen felt old at the time!).

Once I was back, I started every Arsenal game apart from one, where I came off the bench in the second half. I was happy. I was back where I wanted to be, and things were going well. Then, in June 2016, just over a year later, I injured my ankle again. Badly. I thought I knew what would happen next: I thought I could work out when I would be back, that I knew how to fix my ankle with physio, that I had been here before. But that wasn't how things went – this time, I ended up needing surgery. I was out for five months.

Even though this injury was worse than any I'd had before, it felt different. Or maybe a better way of saying it is that the way I felt about it was different. I hoped the surgery would fix my ankle for good so that my injury would be less likely to happen again, and I was more established in the team so I felt better in myself as a player. When I had the first two ankle injuries back-to-back I felt like I still had to prove my worth on the pitch. This time I was thinking: *I've done this. I've been through injuries and I've come back better as a player.* I knew I could recover. So I was more comfortable taking the time my body needed to get back to full fitness.

Now, when I get injured, I'm a lot less worried because I know who I am as a player. I know what my standard is and what I'm working towards during my recovery. Back then, I didn't know where I was going or what I was trying to get back to. I just kept worrying about how I was supposed to be developing as a player, and feeling anxious that I wasn't getting better.

Injuries have made me relax and take things day-by-day, but they've also made me appreciate the good times more because you never know when the next setback will come. It's like that wavy line I was talking about in the last chapter – the lows in life make you appreciate the high points!

Letting go and trusting the process (you'll hear injured footballers say they must 'trust the process' a lot) is not an easy thing to do. I still battle that now. I've learned that because I live and breathe football, it can make me the happiest I'll ever be. But it can break my heart just as quickly. There are so many uncontrollables in football – and this is another thing football players always say:

YOU CAN **ONLY** CONTROL THE CONTROLLABLES

('Controllables' isn't even a real word!).

I love this saying because it means that you have no control over whether someone is going to run down the pitch, take you out with both feet and badly injure you. You have no control over everyone in your team being fit and healthy enough to compete. In other words, you need to learn to let go of the things that you can't control.

That's why my priority is making sure that there are lots of things in life that I can enjoy – even if one day football can't be one of them. What makes me happy away from the pitch is my family, spending time with my teammates and listening to my records. I've learned to live in the moment because you never know what tomorrow will bring.

I injured my ankle again after the Euros, towards the end of 2022, while playing for Arsenal. But I knew what I needed to do because I understood my body and mind so much better. I told my coaches that I needed a break; to be away from the environment at the training ground as part of my recovery. Once you know yourself and learn to let go of what you can't control, you can be more honest with yourself and others about what you need.

Learning to let go and trust the process by not worrying about the possible outcomes has helped me on the pitch too. It's allowed me to just focus on the plan for the team and be the best version of myself I can be. In the quarter-final of the Euros, in our match against Spain, we were 1-0 down with sixteen minutes of normal time left to play. I've heard that a lot of people in the crowd and at home felt nervous – they thought that our time in the tournament was up. Spain were good. Really, *really* good. But I always had this feeling that we would win that game. I just knew, inside me, that our journey wasn't over. I know my teammates felt that way too. The fact that I wasn't worried meant that I could focus. I didn't want to jeopardize the plan and do something that would lead to Spain scoring. I just needed to pay attention, do what I'm good at and try to deliver. I didn't want to force anything to try and make an attack happen.

If I had kept thinking, 'We're 1-0 down, we're 1-0 down, we're 1-0 down', it wouldn't change the score. If you focus on the 'what ifs', too much you get caught up in wanting to do more, to try and make something happen. But if you're giving everything you have, then you can trust the process. If we had lost that game we would have left with no regrets because we gave the match everything we had. Ella Toone scored and normal time finished at 1-1. Then Georgia Stanway scored in extra time. We had done it. It was all part of trusting the process.

As strange as it sounds, it's important to not make what you love your whole entire world. I love playing football, but I've had to work hard to make sure that it's not the focus of my entire life. Being injured has helped me with this, because it's a reminder that you could easily have to step away from the game forever. What if I got an injury that I couldn't come back from?

That's why not being solely reliant on football is really important to me. Like I said, when I'm injured I have time to do other things, like listening to music (yes, I love music), going to visit projects that Arsenal run in the community and travelling. All of these things remind me just how much I love football, why I shouldn't take it for granted or waste any time not enjoying it.

One of the things that has helped me to keep calm when I'm injured, is studying to be an accountant. I know that football might not always be there, so I have accountancy as a plan B. I've always really enjoyed maths, and this is a good way to spend time doing other things I enjoy, and showing myself that there are loads of other things I can be good at.

I like accountancy and I like maths now, but to be honest, I haven't always found things easy when it comes to studying. I really struggled with the leap-up from GCSE level to A-Levels. Changing schools and taking on new challenges can be really tough, but I want you to know that there are people around you who can help to support you during those times, until you find your feet.

Football has helped me to be patient, trust myself, trust the process and not think too far ahead. I wish I'd had that in my head at school. Because, when you think about it, worrying about exams is as much wasted effort as worrying about a result of a football match. I know that if my team work hard on the training pitch we'll be in the best position to win, and it's the same with school. If you work hard, aim to do a little bit better and a little bit more than you did the day before, then, whatever happens in the exam, you will know that you gave it the very best you possibly could. And there's nothing more you can do than that.

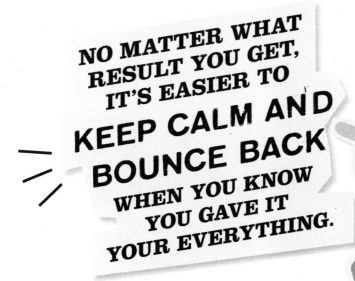

NO MATTER WHAT RESULT YOU GET, IT'S EASIER TO KEEP CALM AND BOUNCE BACK WHEN YOU KNOW YOU GAVE IT YOUR EVERYTHING.

[5]

Teamwork & Leadership

I am so proud to be England captain. It's a massive honour to wear the armband and lead the team out onto the pitch at the start of each game, and I love that it gives me more opportunities to speak about the things that I believe in. But, as much as I love it, one thing I don't like is when people say that being captain is a big achievement. It's really just an extension of my regular job and responsibilities. Of course, it's nice to feel like your manager trusts you, but really, anyone in any team could be the captain. Look at me, for instance – I'm not the captain of Arsenal, but I am the captain of England.

Every manager will want something different from their captain. They might want someone who thinks the same way as them, or who understands their tactics inside out. But they could also want someone who is the complete opposite to them, to make sure that there is a balance of personalities in the team's leadership.

I had only played six minutes of football in a major tournament for England before Sarina asked me to be captain; just before the start of the Euro 2022 tournament. In many ways, I wasn't the obvious choice. There were lots of players in the squad who had far more experience than I had. Some had been captain of their club teams, and others who had even captained the England team before! Even though I was the captain, everyone in the team felt the responsibility to lead together. I really think that's one reason why we won the Euros: the more you give to other people, the more you get back and the more successful you become as a team.

YOU REALLY CAN'T DO IT ON YOUR OWN.

Being the captain doesn't make you a superhero, but it does give you the power to lift other people up. It's the same outside of football too. Being a prefect, a member of the student council, or the captain of any team or club at school doesn't make you better than any of your classmates, just like being a boss at work doesn't make you better than the people you work with.

The thing that I like most about being a leader, is being able to have a positive impact on others. We spend our whole lives chasing things that will help make us happy. And the best way to make yourself feel good is to make someone else feel good about themselves and confident in their own abilities. As a leader, this is one of your biggest responsibilities.

When you're in a position of power – like being a captain – your job is to bring out the best in other people. But this is something everyone on a football pitch should be doing regardless, not just the captain. When you support each other in a team, you will find that you can accomplish so much more. It's not just the captain's job to ensure everyone is working together. If I can help people to be their best selves, the whole will benefit, including me.

In 2015, I ended up in a really unusual situation. I was part of the England Under-19's team and we were playing games that would decide whether or not we would qualify for the Euros later that year. We were drawn in a group with Norway, Northern Ireland and Switzerland. In our first game of the qualifiers, we were playing against Norway.

By the time ninety minutes of normal play was up, we were losing, 2-1. We went into added time and the team and I were desperately trying everything we could to score. In the ninety-sixth minute, just moments before the end of the game, Rosella Ayane was fouled in the box and we were given a penalty. I wasn't the captain, but I was the penalty taker. That was my responsibility within the team. If I scored, we would draw, but if I missed we would lose and be in a bad position in the group which meant possibly not making the Euros!

It was a lot of pressure. We had one last chance not to lose the game and it was on me to score. I stepped up to take the penalty and . . . I scored it. But, something else happened too. Just as I was about to kick the ball, it turned out that Rosella had moved into the penalty box. If a player moves into the penalty area before the ball is kicked, it's called an encroachment, which is against the rules. So, the referee blew the whistle and ruled the goal out. I went to put the ball on the spot to retake it, but instead, they gave Norway a free kick! We had lost the opportunity to score, and we ended up losing to Norway 2-1. It was so gutting.

Thankfully, people realized that the referee had made a mistake. In that situation, the referee was supposed to make me retake the penalty. So, five days later, we had to replay the game from the time of my penalty, the ninety-sixth minute. We only found out our appeal against the decision had been successful the day before. I cried in the dressing room under the stress of it all. I knew that our chances in the tournament rested on one penalty that I had to take! But, Katie Zelem told me that I was the one person she would choose for that situation and that made me feel more confident. Rosella offered to stay up on the halfway line, to be on the safe side!

In that moment, waiting to take the penalty, I understood that if I took all the pressure and responsibility on my own shoulders then I would be downplaying the role of everybody else in the team who had helped to put me there and prepared me for that moment. My teammates made me feel like that too – they knew that whether we won or lost that game, it wasn't on me, because we had all played this match together. There were ninety-six minutes of football before my penalty that we had all played together. So the pressure that I was feeling went from being as heavy as the weight of the world, with the team and fans, expectations all on me as an individual, to a lighter feeling of shared responsibility. Win or lose, I was only one part of a big team.

I can remember the feeling of slowly walking up to the spot to take the penalty. I was nervous but tried to stay calm. I'd spent a long time knowing that the entire game would be decided on my one kick. I took a deep breath – and then – I scored!

We held on for the final sixteen seconds and won the game.

In my football career so far, I have played with lots of different captains. At Arsenal, there was the incredible striker, Kelly Smith. She was so talented on the pitch, and that made you want to be the best you could be so that you wouldn't let her down. Alex Scott was an immense defender. As a captain, she made me think about who I was as a person and what I had to offer the team. She managed to squeeze every extra ounce out of me. Steph Houghton was the England captain before me, and she was ultra-professional and respected by all, because she didn't leave any stone unturned – she would do everything possible to make sure the team was as prepared as we could be.

My captain at Arsenal is Scottish midfielder, Kim Little. She is all of those things mixed together. A supremely talented football player, Kim is one of the best to ever play. She is super professional and someone who will challenge you to be better. Kim hasn't just helped me to be a better player though, I've also learned so much from her about being a captain too. I can see all the time and energy she has invested into me as a player and a person. And now that I know more about what being a captain means, I think about how I can help support her, when I'm at Arsenal. She's never says: 'I'm the captain, you sit down, be quiet and listen to me.' She gives me the space to help and to voice my opinions.

THAT'S THE SIGN OF A **GOOD LEADER** someone who is able to **BRING OUT THE BEST IN OTHER PEOPLE** in their team.

The first great captains in my life though, were my mum and grandma. I was very lucky to have two women in my family who were both so sporty. They played badminton, netball and football back when it was a lot harder for women to do sport.

In 1921, the Football Association decided that football was an unsuitable sport for women, and women were pretty much banned from playing, even though it had been a popular sport at the time. Just one year earlier, 53,000 people had watched a game between Dick Kerr Ladies and St Helen's, at Everton's ground Goodison Park! The ban was lifted in 1971, not long before my mum started playing, although a lot of people still thought girls shouldn't play football. At first, my mum had to pretend she was a boy to be able to play, because no one would let a girl join a football club!

Later on, she played for Milton Keynes Town and was part of the team that knocked Arsenal Women out of the FA Cup. She scored and provided an assist (which means she helped to set up another goal)! This was long before I was born, but she doesn't let me forget it. My mum and my grandma showed me what standing up for yourself means; they pushed against what was considered normal for girls to do and they challenged me to do the same.

That's why they are my first great captains, because inspiring and challenging those around you to be better is exactly what good captains do.

There is always a lot of expectation on the captain of a team. At the Euros, I tried very hard to not have expectations about what sort of captain I should be. It was important to me to be myself and to not try and change into what I thought a good captain looked like. Somebody will always have to go onto the pitch wearing an armband – that's just a fact. And if that person is me, it doesn't change who I am. And it shouldn't ever change you, either.

Being asked to be captain also didn't mean I suddenly had all the answers or never made mistakes. Part of being a leader is knowing that it's okay to be vulnerable and to ask others for help or advice when you need it. We learn from each other all the time and are better for it. One of the most important things we did at the Euros was to walk out onto the pitch wanting to have fun, be ourselves and try our best. And we could do that because we had all supported and learned from each other along the way.

As well as leading the squad out onto the pitch before every game, as captain you sometimes have to speak on behalf of the team. Being captain has made me reflect a lot on what I do and say. You're always aware that more people are watching you and listening to your voice. I had to do lots of interviews during the Euros, on TV, in newspapers, in live press conferences and I needed to make sure that I reflected my team's views and not just my own.

THAT IS WHY LISTENING AND BEING OPEN WITH EACH OTHER IS SO IMPORTANT.

We do a lot of team events, social events and team building exercises, to bring us closer together as the England team. This also helps us to understand each other better. If you know what your friend or teammate's biggest strengths and weaknesses are, you will be able to spot when they are struggling. In turn, you'll be able to help them. If you care about the person next to you, you are going to fight for each other that little bit more.

We are all leaders, even if you don't wear a captain's armband. And as a leader, you need to listen to and trust yourself. You need to be yourself and learn from people around you, rather than try to be someone else. You are in charge of your own life, your own journey and how you treat people on that journey. You can decide to take on responsibility and help to lift others up the way you want to be lifted up, and you don't need a title to be able to do that. I'm trying to do that as a captain, but I tried before as a member of the team too. You can act like a leader in all your relationships, whether that's at home or school; by helping those around you to be the best versions of themselves.

LIFE IS MADE UP OF

TEAMS

YOUR FAMILY,

YOUR FRIENDS,

YOUR CLASS,

YOUR SCHOOL,

AND WE WILL ALL BE
BETTER OFF IF WE

WORK

TOGETHER

[6]

Allyship, Inclusivity & Representation

Three months after we became European champions, we played the USA – the world champions – at Wembley in October 2022. We won 2-1. It was a great game, in front of a huge crowd of fans. Tickets had sold out in less than 24 hours, which made it the fastest-selling England game (men's or women's!) at Wembley, since the first match at the stadium in 2007.

During that time, some very special things happened. The first special moment was when the original Lionesses came down to watch

us train. They had played in England's first official match in 1972 against Scotland, after the ban was lifted.

At our match against the USA, this group of phenomenal women were given official England caps for the first time. A player's 'caps' refers to the amount of international matches they've played in. You get given a cap – yes, an actual hat! – for every game. That's why when you ask how many games a player has played for their country you ask how many caps they've got. (I don't keep many of my caps or trophies or medals myself. I keep the most valuable ones locked up but I send most home to my mum.) I play football to make my family proud, so that feels right.

It was really important for our team to meet and say thank you to those players. They had helped fight to get the ban on women's football lifted and played for England when many people didn't think women should be allowed to play.

We had won the Euros, but we wouldn't have been able to do that without help from all of the England players that had come before us. If they hadn't fought to do what they loved I might not have been able to be a professional football player fifty years later. They put down a ladder for us to climb.

I want to do the same thing for the people who come after me. I want you to have the opportunity to do whatever it is that you want in life; whether you want to play football or do something completely different. I want you to have opportunities and options. The way I see it is: if you choose *not* to play football that is a good thing, because it means you had the choice in the first place! And I want you to think about how you can help make what you're passionate about easier, safer and more inclusive for everyone coming after you.

After playing as the only girl in a boys' team when I was younger, getting to play in mixed and girls' teams was amazing. I went from walking into training or a match feeling different and standing out, to feeling like I wasn't alone any more. Being surrounded by people who want you to succeed creates a strong bond and a really positive environment. It becomes a safe space. You know that you're not going to have someone at any minute turn around and tell you that you shouldn't be there. Instead, you turn up to play football in an environment that encourages you.

FOOTBALL IS A REALLY POWERFUL SPORT.

People all over the world love both playing football and watching football, and they are very passionate about it. One of the things that makes it so popular is that it is very easy for people to play because it doesn't involve lots of expensive equipment.

All you need is a ball and something to use as goalposts – and that could be jumpers, bags, chalk . . . whatever you have around!

Everyone knows the basic rules: you have two teams trying to put the ball in the opposite goal. You can even go out onto a football pitch, not actually say anything to anyone and still play the game. (I wouldn't recommend that though!) That's what is special about football, it brings anyone and everyone together. You can speak different languages and come from different places in the world, but on the football pitch, none of that matters.

In life, when we connect with people, it's usually pretty natural: you talk and share with someone, and they either understand who you are as a person or they don't. When you play football, the people next to you already understand you, without talking, because you all share a common love and a common language: football. You don't have to try too hard to find common ground because you already have one, you all enjoy doing the same thing. You are already connected. Everyone is welcome on the football pitch.

No matter whether you want to play or you want to watch, no one is excluded.

Anyone can play football – no matter your race or background, it doesn't matter whether you're big or small, fast or slow, able-bodied or disabled, gay or straight. You can play.

Right now, women's football is a welcoming and safe environment because lots of the people involved in it understand what it feels like to not feel very welcome. But we're all working towards a point where people look at us and say 'those girls are so good!' instead of 'those girls have done so well considering what they've had to go through.' A point where the next generation of players coming up can bond over their shared love of football and not because they've ever been made to feel unwelcome anywhere else.

REPRESENTATION REALLY MATTERS.

If women's football players are visible, it means you are seeing women doing amazing things. It is important that our games are shown on TV and that you get to see us out there playing football, doing what we want to do, because hopefully you will feel that you can do it too. When I went into school nobody knew any women footballers. Now, I hope you go into school and people are talking about Alessia Russo and Beth Mead's goals as much as they are about Harry Kane and Lionel Messi's.

Hopefully we can inspire you to believe that you can do whatever you want to to – football or no football. Football is far from the only thing women and girls have felt excluded from. There aren't enough women in positions of power, in politics or running top companies, which means that a lot of important decisions are made, including things that affect women, that women don't have enough of a say in.

Our Euros win wasn't just to inspire the next generation of female footballers, or the next generation of football fans to be more accepting of girls playing. I hope that everyone can look at what we do and feel empowered to do whatever they want to do. Inclusivity is very, very important. Having a group of people, in a sports team or in any team, who come from lots of different backgrounds means better decisions, as many diverse experiences can be represented and heard.

Women's football is very welcoming, but we still have a long way to go to make it the best and most inclusive place it can be. If you watched us win the Euros, then you will have seen that all of our players who started that game were white. I want all children to be able to look at our team and feel represented, no matter their race. Certainly, there have been many brilliant Black players that have played for the Lionesses senior side: Rachel Yankey, Alex Scott, Hope Powell, Mary Phillip, Anita Asante, Eniola Aluko, Lianne Sanderson, Danielle Carter, Demi Stokes, Nikita Parris, Jess Carter, Kerry Davis, Lauren James – to name only a few! But we recognise that we need to do better. We need to make it easier for girls from different backgrounds to access football.

While football can be played anywhere, there are some barriers to getting into professional football. Up until recently, lots of the academies for women's teams had moved out of city centres which are more diverse, to smaller towns around the cities which are less so. That made them harder and more expensive to get to for a lot of young players. For instance, if a parent works more than one job or works long shifts, it can be both expensive and take time they don't have for them to get their daughter to these clubs.

Because of the work and support of lots of people, seventy new training centres for girls, and women's football in towns and cities are opening up to make it easier and more accessible for any girl who wants to play football. This is a great step for making football more inclusive.

It's so important to fight for your own opportunities in life, but it's also really important that you fight for each other too.

You can be a brilliant ally to your friends no matter their gender, ethnicity, religion, size or whether they are differently-abled. An ally is someone who supports something that they aren't directly affected by. I'm a white woman with privilege, but I want to do my best to help everyone have better access to football.

We need people from outside of women's football to stick up for and believe in it. Women's football has been able to grow because it has good allies.

Arsenal legend Ian Wright is a brilliant ally for women's football. He has done a lot to promote it. He talks about our games on TV and podcasts and he oozes passion for it. He often wears shirts with the names of the women players on instead of players from the men's team. A lot of people who probably wouldn't usually watch women's football follow Ian Wright and when they hear him talk about women's football with so much enthusiasm, some will definitely think, 'maybe I'll give this a try'.

That's what I want. I want everyone, everywhere, to give our games a chance and have the opportunity to fall in love with women's football. The more people that are involved, the bigger and better the women's game gets and the more opportunities people have to enjoy this inclusive and supportive space, that welcomes anyone and everyone.

[]

European Champions

I always said to myself that during the Euros in 2022 I would embrace every emotion, good or bad. I wanted to feel every moment. I wanted to enjoy every high and if that meant feeling the lows too, then it was worth it. I wanted to be present. I didn't want to switch off to just get through it.

If you watched the final, you will have seen me crying my eyes out at the end. I felt so relieved, but the emotions were so strong I felt like I was falling apart, into little pieces. We worked so, *so* hard to reach that final game against Germany.

The noise had been so loud around the final, but we managed to stay in a little bubble throughout the tournament. We tried to shut out the outside world, tune out from what fans were saying, what was being said on TV and in newspapers, and just focus on us and what we could control, it was all about *controlling the controllables* (remember that phrase?). It's impossible not to feel the expectation when you walk out in front of 87,192 fans. I soaked up all that atmosphere. I thought I was going to cry, but instead I smiled the whole way through the national anthem.

But it was almost a disaster for me early on. Twenty-six minutes into the game, the ball came into our box and I blocked it in front of the goal. But my clearance bounced off a couple of players and then it hit me on the shoulder. My arms were out, not by my side, so the referee thought it might have been a handball. The moment was replayed by the video assistant referee to check if it was indeed a foul. None of my teammates had seen what had happened and they were all confused. Rachel Daly asked me what they were checking for and I said, 'it's for me'. My heart sunk. I couldn't believe what was happening. I was the captain of England in the final of the Euros at Wembley and I might have given away a penalty? It felt like time had slowed down whilst we waited to hear the decision. When the check finally ended without giving a penalty, I was on top of the world and I actually think that helped me to relax and enjoy the game more. One of the worst things that could have happened, didn't.

In the fifty-fifth minute, with the game still goalless, our manager Sarina brought on Ella Toone and Alessia Russo. They had been so impactful coming off the bench throughout the competition and seven minutes later Keira Walsh sent a perfect long ball for Tooney to run onto. She chipped it over the German goalkeeper, Merle Frohms, and scored. We held onto that lead for seventeen minutes but then Lina Magull scored to level things out! The game went to extra time. We had half an hour to win, or we would go to penalties. We were tired, but we couldn't give up. I don't remember this, but Lauren Hemp says that I pointed at my chest and told her to play with her heart and not her head. That's what we were all trying to do, to focus and play with our hearts, and not overthink things. Lauren did just that. She sent in a perfect cross from a corner kick and Chloe Kelly scored!

I didn't even see who had scored in the moment, I just saw a foot stick out, the ball go in and then everyone went wild, celebrating! It was such an amazing feeling. But I couldn't let myself get too carried away . . . We still had a job to do. We had to keep our lead. To do that, it was time to play with our heads, and switch our tactics to ensure that Germany couldn't score again.

Like I said, at the final whistle I was a wreck. I had been bombarded by emotion after emotion not just for the length of the game, but for the whole tournament! When you achieve something that you've worked so hard for, suddenly you realize all of the difficult choices and decisions that you've made throughout your entire life feel justified. Even the wrong ones. Because every single one, right or wrong, helped to get you to that moment. They helped you to win.

Don't get me wrong, you don't need to win to feel like the hard work is justified. Football gives me so much even if my team loses, but winning is the icing on the cake. The German team worked hard too, but England just ended up in a situation where we were the winners that day. Does that mean all the little decisions Germany made weren't justified and worth it? No. Winning the right way is important too, you don't win to spite someone else.

I would never want to be part of an arrogant team that doesn't respect their opposition.

A gold medal and a major trophy win are very *very* special. Every football player wants to win things, that's your job when you're on the pitch, but I think the most satisfying thing about winning the Euros was that it expanded our platform to do great things on and off the pitch. What do I mean when I talk about us having a platform? Think of a platform as being like a stage in a theatre. Before the Euros, we were stood on a tiny stage, with a small audience. Now, we're on a much bigger stage with a much larger audience, because people started to get excited and wanted to watch and follow us. That means more people know about women's football, follow our team, and listen to us when we speak. That makes our voices and what we say even more powerful.

The last time England were in a Euros final, we lost 6-2 to Germany. That was in 2009, long before I was in the team. The big difference back then was that the German team had received a lot of support – lots of the players were professional players and able to train every day. As funding for women's football in England wasn't as strong, most of the England team were only part-time. That meant they were training and playing matches around working and studying because they were far less supported than we are today. It took lots of years of many people's hard work to get the Lionesses back to a Euros final and this time we weren't massive underdogs because lots had been done to give us the best chance to succeed. That's why it is frustrating when people say that women's football needs to get big crowds *before* it deserves investment.

You can't expect a plant to grow without watering it and caring for it first.

I want you to grow and thrive, and that is why I want you to have the opportunity and support to do whatever you are passionate about. I like having a platform to be able to support women's sport but, more than that, I like being able to speak up for *you* and demand better for *you* and to help make you believe that *your* voice matters.

Being part of a winning team has made me feel more able to do that. We proved ourselves and we've shown that investing in girls and women is worth it. We've never asked for a lot as players, all we want is to be able to compete at the top level, bring others up with us and to be given the support and tools we need to achieve that.

If somebody raises the stakes, then everybody else either must choose to follow and compete, or stay where they are. That's a beautiful thing because it means we all push each other and help each other to grow. Some of the nicest messages I got after we won the Euros were from American players, even though we are now more competitive and closer to challenging them to become the world's best team. They understood the impact of winning like we did. In 1999, they had a similar moment when they won the World Cup in the US in front of over 90,000 fans. That World Cup win rocketed the profile of women's football in their country, in the same way that the Euros win has put women's football on the map in England.

Our win has empowered so many people, but it's also empowered us. I'm empowered by the energy that I get back from everybody else, from a kid so excited to tell me about their team, or a mum telling me about how much we've inspired their child, to an older woman saying they've started playing walking football! That's why when the Euros was finished we did something a little different. The day after the final we went to Trafalgar Square in the middle of London with the trophy for a big party with thousands of fans. We got back on the coach, and everyone was so happy. Lotte Wubben-Moy, my teammate at Arsenal and England, suggested then we write a letter calling on the government to provide equal access to football in schools – so that every girl and every boy can play football in school if they want to.

We had started talking a bit about what we wanted our legacy to be before the final. We wanted to do something real. So, when Lotte suggested the letter, I was excited. I agreed, 'This is exactly what we should do.' If we want our legacy from the Euros to be more than just winning, we need to change things for the better. And we won't let that demand for equal access slide, we will keep working to make it happen. Then, hopefully, when people asked us how things changed after our win, we can show them in real numbers exactly how many more girls are able to play football because of us.

I've already talked a little but about how I grew during the Euros. We all did. With each win our confidence expanded, we became more focused, and we were more comfortable and trusting of our abilities on the pitch as a result. I really grew into my captaincy role, off the pitch too. Before the final I had to do the press conference with Sarina. The press conference room at Wembley was PACKED with journalists and TV cameras. I could have just said that I was excited for the game and talked about the preparation and the pressure . . . but the whole world was watching and this was an opportunity to say so much more. I told them that the Euros had already changed women's football and society regardless of whether we won or lost the next day. I said that the final was just the start of the journey rather than the end of one. I also spoke about how I hoped that every success we had would open the eyes of somebody who maybe didn't view women as equal to men. That came from the heart. I was honest, and the reception to what I said made me feel like I was in touch with the way others were feeling too, especially with the rest of my teammates. It really felt like we could improve things.

That's what we all wanted to do, CHANGE THE WORLD, that's what we felt capable of doing in that moment.

We have changed things already. I can see that from the crowds we are drawing at Women's Super League games. Now our England games sell out quickly! One dad told me that he had been running his daughter's football team, but now he had to organize seven teams because so many girls wanted to play. He said, 'girls just kept turning up and I kept having to make new teams!' It's stories like that which make my heart swell and show me that we have made a difference. We want you to decide to go out, pick up a pair of boots and lace up. You might never want to be a footballer, but I didn't want to be a gymnast. I did it because it gave me skills that I wouldn't have gotten elsewhere. There's probably been plenty of times you've not wanted to go to school, right? But ultimately you know it's going to benefit you in some way. And, I hope that all of you who have decided that you want to be involved in football will have felt a bit more empowered walking up the length of the pitch. I hope you feel like it has enriched your life in different ways.

There's a phrase that's used a lot around women's football: *if you can't see it, you can't be it.*

One of the most powerful things that we can do as players is exist in the public eye – just seeing women performing at the top level can help others believe that they can get there too. I hope that if you go into school and say, 'I'm going to be a footballer', nobody thinks that's silly because everyone, parents and carers and teachers and kids, knows now that you can be.

Women's football has a bright future. I don't like to look backwards and dwell on the negativity and struggles of the past because I can't change those things. The only reason I look back is to learn from the past and work out how to make things better moving forward.

If you got a bad grade at school last year, what's a better use of your energy, being sad about that grade or working out how you can do better next time? It's a no-brainer.

It's the same with football matches, we take them game by game. You don't go, 'Oh we lost this game last year so we're probably going to lose it again.' You go, 'We lost this one last year because of X, Y, and Z and we don't want to be in that position again, so we're going to do this differently now.'

Football players talk about winning being addictive, but I *think* it's the feeling of getting better that we are really chasing. I've talked a lot about *controlling the controllables*. Well this is it. This is your life and *you* are in control of improving yourself. You may not be able to completely change the world, or the people around you, but you can control you. So dream big, follow your passions and chase your goals.

BECAUSE YOU HAVE THE POWER

THE TEN RULES FOR BELIEVING IN YOURSELF

1. Love yourself and be your own best cheerleader.

2. Embrace the things that make you unique.

3. Don't be afraid to do the things you love.

4. Push yourself outside your comfort zone.

5. Don't measure your success against other people.

6. Allow yourself to be vulnerable. It's a strength, not a weakness.

7. Don't be afraid of big risks. They mean big rewards.

8. Only attempt to control the controllables.

9. Don't just fight for your own success, help to raise others up, too.

10. Trust the process and back yourself.

About the Authors

Leah Williamson plays as a defender for Arsenal and is the captain of the England Women's Football team.

In the summer of 2022 Leah led the Lionesses to victory in the UEFA Women's Euro 2022, the first captain in the men's or women's senior teams to lead England to a European victory.

Suzanne Wrack is a women's football writer for *The Guardian*, who has previously worked for BBC Sport, *The Sunday Times* and *Trinity Mirror* (now Reach PLC). She is passionate about sport and enjoys exploring the politics of sport, and has an interest in fan-owned football clubs and issues around discrimination in sport.

Suzanne is on the expert panel which helps determine the Women's Super League player of the month and is on the selection panel for the Women's Super League Hall of Fame. She has a chapter included in *Football, She Wrote*, an anthology of women's football writers published in September 2021 on Chelsea manager Emma Hayes and is the author of *A Woman's Game – The rise, fall and rise again of women's football and Strong Women*. She is the co-writer of Lioness captain Leah Williamson's debut book, *You Have the Power*.

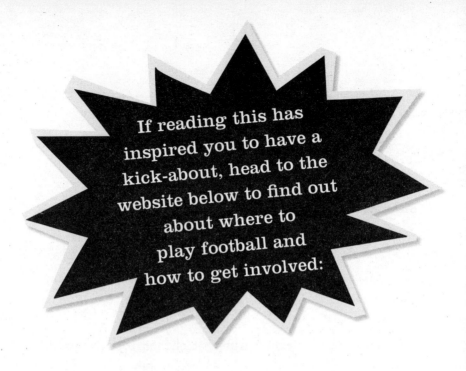

If reading this has inspired you to have a kick-about, head to the website below to find out about where to play football and how to get involved:

www.englandfootball.com/participate